Hurricane!

By Carol M. Elliott

46921_004

Scott Foresman
is an imprint of

Glenview, Illinois • Boston, Massachusetts • Chandler, Arizona •
Upper Saddle River, New Jersey

Photographs

Every effort has been made to secure permission and provide appropriate credit for photographic material. The publisher deeply regrets any omission and pledges to correct errors called to its attention in subsequent editions.

Unless otherwise acknowledged, all photographs are the property of Pearson Education, Inc.

Photo locators denoted as follows: Top (T), Center (C), Bottom (B), Left (L), Right (R), Background (Bkgd)

ISBN 13: 978-0-328-46912-3
ISBN 10:   0-328-46912-2

3 4 5 6 7 8 9 10 V010 13 12 11 10

Watch out, Florida! Here comes a big storm!

The storm will get bigger. The winds will blow faster. The rain will fall harder. It will become a hurricane!

Most hurricanes drop 6 to 12 inches of rain. That's a lot of rain at one time. Homes may get flooded.

Hurricanes are huge. A hurricane can be more than one hundred miles wide.

Scientists watch each hurricane. They predict where it will hit land.

It isn't safe to stay home in a hurricane. People leave in cars and buses. They go to safer places.

Hurricane Katrina was one of the worst hurricanes in the United States. It hit Louisiana, Mississippi, and Alabama in August of 2005. Its winds blew more than 140 miles per hour.

Hurricane Katrina flooded cities and towns. More than a million people lost their homes.

Hurricane Ike hit Texas in September of 2008. Its winds blew more than 110 miles per hour.

Hurricane Ike dropped 12 inches of rain in some places. Many homes and buildings were flooded.

A hurricane is much more than a big wind. It brings rain, giant waves, and lots of water. It can change people's lives forever.